Slammin' Simon's
20 Essential Drum Rudiments

check out all the guides at
SlamminSimon.com

say hello at **slamminsimon@gmail.com**

© copyright 2017 Mark Powers
Simon and Rudi illustrations by Autumn Linde

Slammin' Simon plays . . .

practice pads

VIC FIRTH
drumsticks

is a member of the . . .

PERCUSSIVE
ARTS SOCIETY

and reads . . .

MODERNDRUMMER
magazine

ROLL RUDIMENTS

Single Stroke Roll 8
Single Stroke Four 10
Single Stroke Seven 13
Double Stroke Roll 15
5-Stroke Roll 16
9-Stroke Roll 19
17-Stroke Roll 20

DIDDLE RUDIMENTS

Single Paradiddle 23
Double Paradiddle 25
Triple Paradiddle 27
Paradiddle-diddle 30

MORE ROLL RUDIMENTS

Triple Stroke Roll 34
Multiple Bounce Roll 35

FLAM RUDIMENTS

Flam 42
Flam Tap 47
Flam Accent 48
Swiss Army Triplet 49

DRAG RUDIMENTS

Drag 52
Drag Paradiddle #1 57
Single Ratamacue 59

Hey there – and thanks for checking out this guide
to my 20 Essential Drum Rudiments!

My name is Simon and, as you probably guessed,
I'm a drummer. My nickname is Slammin' Simon and
I've got a super cool pet turtle named Rudi. We
love showing drummers just like you all
kinds of cool rhythms and techniques.

Rudi's name is short for the word "rudiment."
Rudiments are basic drum hand patterns
(or "stickings") that every drummer should
learn . . . and rudiments are exactly
what this book is all about!

There is an awesome group of drummers called the Percussive Arts Society (or the PAS), and they put together a list of the most important drum rudiments to learn. The PAS calls their list the 40 International Drum Rudiments. You're going to learn half of those in this guide, a list that Rudi and I call the 20 Essential Drum Rudiments.

These rudiments are divided into four sections:

Roll Rudiments

Diddle Rudiments

Flam Rudiments

Drag Rudiments

• • •

Rolls? Diddles? Flams? Drags?

Those might just seem like silly made-up words but they are actually very cool patterns that sound great once you know how to play them! The rudiments will have us combining our right and left hands in all sorts of ways, creating some awesome patterns that we can play on any kind of drum or percussion instrument that we'd like.

Ready to jump in?

So are we! Grab your drumsticks, get settled
in at your practice pad or snare drum,
and let's get started.

• • •

When reading the music in this book, you'll often
see the letters R and L written below some
of our music notes. The letter tells you which
drumstick should play the note that's above it.

R = play a note with the stick in your RIGHT hand

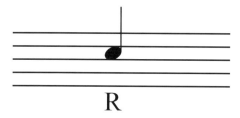

R

L = play a note with the stick in your LEFT hand

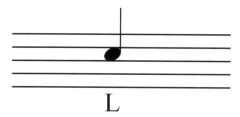

L

Easy enough, right?

ROLL RUDIMENTS

You've probably heard drummers play
super fast bursts of notes before, back and forth
between their two sticks. Those are sometimes
called "rolls" and are what we're going to
start off learning how to play first!

SINGLE STROKE ROLL

Our first rudiment is the Single Stroke Roll,
which is exactly what its name suggests:
single strokes (or one note per hand) played over
and over again, from hand to hand. One right
hit, one left hit, a right, and a left, then right, left,
right, left . . . I think you get the idea.

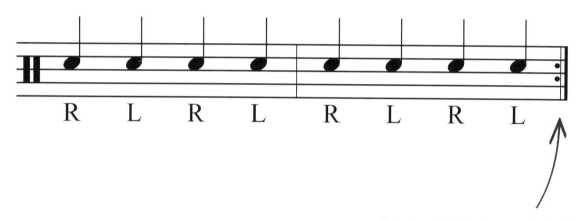

this is called a "repeat sign"
and means to go back and
start again at the beginning

Begin very slowly, alternating between rights and
lefts, using only your wrists to play (not bending
from your elbows), and make sure both hands create
notes that sound the same.

Don't let your strong hand play harder (or louder)
than your weak hand. Keep on repeating the single
strokes, without speeding up, until you feel
very comfortable with the pattern. Stay loose
and relaxed as you play.

Once you've played this rudiment nice and slowly for a while, and they sound even and smooth, you can gradually start going a little bit faster. But not TOO fast. Only speed up a little bit at a time and be sure that, as your single strokes get faster, they still stay steady and you still stay relaxed.

RUDI TIP:

If you start to tense up, or your notes get choppy and uneven, slow down and keep repeating at a more comfortable speed.

This won't be its absolute fastest today, but practice the single stroke roll for a few minutes every day, every week, every month, and you'll eventually have them up to lightning speed!

SINGLE STROKE FOUR

Let's keep playing single strokes but, this time, only a short blast of four of them. Just right, left, right, left. Then a tiny pause. Then right, left, right, left. Pause. And repeat.

To get our timing just perfect, we're going to say the word "triplet" (which is what we drummers sometimes call a grouping of three notes) and play notes along with the sounds our mouth makes.

First, break the word up into three parts and say it out loud several times in a row, smoothly looping the three sections: "tri - pl - et - tri - pl - et"

Now, play notes on your drum or practice pad, perfectly matching the first four syllables you speak: "tri - pl - et - tri" and then DON'T play as you continue speaking the last two: "pl - et"

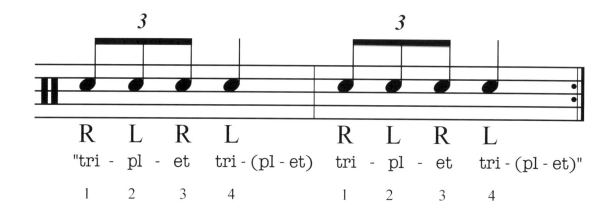

Keep repeating saying and playing that until it starts to flow well, and you feel the rhythm created by the notes and the space at the end of the pattern. Speed up little by little, but remember to slow down if things get tricky . . . or if you get tongue-tied and can't spit out the word "triplet" fast enough yet :)

As drummers, we want to be able to play most rudiments and rhythms starting with either hand. To gain strength, coordination, speed and control, it's important that we give equal attention to both hands.

Since we've only played our Single Stroke Fours with our right hand leading so far, let's go back and play them again, but this time with our left hand leading.

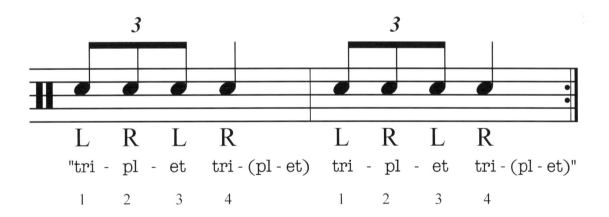

Even though we're starting with our left hand, your goal should be to make these sound identical to our original RLRL sticking.

RUDI'S CHALLENGE

Can you combine our two Single Stroke Four stickings, starting one with the right hand and then one with the left?

Still leave the pause between each phrase, to keep our rhythm and timing correct. Take your time!

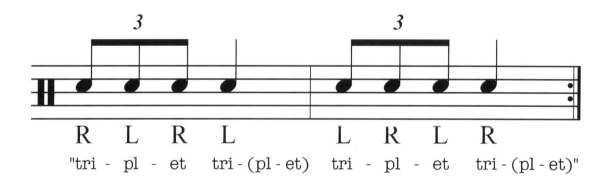

Got that one down?
Good, then the next one's going to be cake!

SINGLE STROKE SEVEN

Very similar to the Single Stroke Four, our next rudiment, the Single Stroke Seven, is based on single strokes, but, you guessed it: seven of them. We'll again use our word "triplet" to help us play the rhythm juuuuust right. This time, we're playing more notes than before (seven, of course) and again leaving a short pause (or rest) after them.

Speak the triplets nice and loud and steady, play the notes right where they're supposed to fall, and you are going to nail these without a problem!

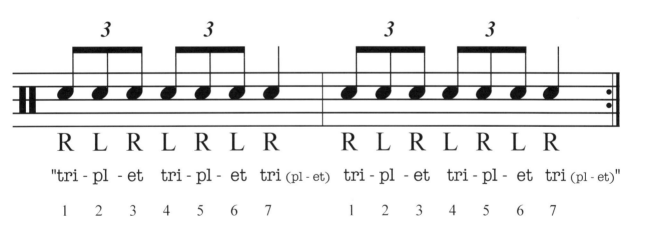

Was I right? Nice job, you!

Just like we did with the Single Stroke Four, let's also play these with our left hand beginning.

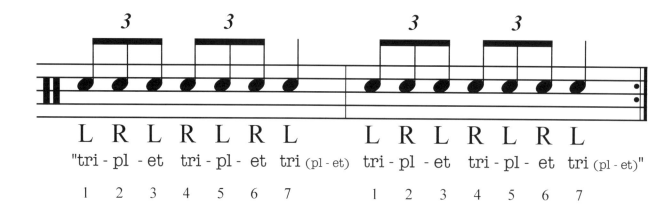

L R L R L R L

"tri - pl - et   tri - pl - et   tri (pl - et)   tri - pl - et   tri - pl - et   tri (pl - et)"

1   2   3   4   5   6   7   1   2   3   4   5   6   7

Earlier, Rudi challenged you to combine the
Single Stroke Four stickings (right hand starting and
then left hand starting). Let's do the same here
with our Single Stroke Sevens.

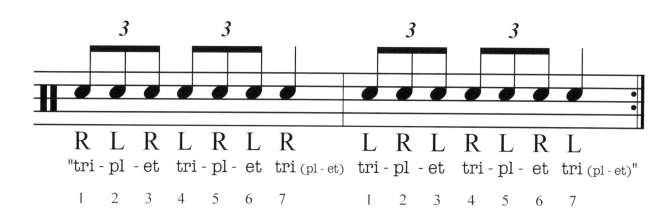

R L R L R L R   L R L R L R L

"tri - pl - et   tri - pl - et   tri (pl - et)   tri - pl - et   tri - pl - et   tri (pl - et)"

1   2   3   4   5   6   7   1   2   3   4   5   6   7

Wow, impressive work on our first three rudiments!
It's time to have some fun and double things up a bit.
And by double, I mean that instead of playing
ONE note per hand, back and forth, we're now
going to play TWO notes per hand, back and forth.

DOUBLE STROKE ROLL

Bending at the wrists, strike two times with your
right drumstick, and then two times with your left
drumstick. Loop that many times
(right, right, left, left, right, right, left, left)
and keep all the notes really even.

Rudi likes to count "1-2, 1-2" as he's playing the
Double Stroke Roll, to make sure he doesn't skip a
note with either hand. Personally, I think it's fun
to say our names while playing them: "Si-mon, Ru-di."
It helps me keep all of the notes super steady. Try
those (or "Right Right Left Left," or the word "double")
and use whatever works best for you.
Better yet, make up your own way to count along!

SAY >> THIS R R L L R R L L

OR >> "1 - 2 1 - 2 1 - 2 1 - 2"

OR >> "Si - mon Ru - di Si - mon Ru - di"

OR >> "dou - ble dou - ble dou - ble dou - ble"

<< OR
WRITE
YOUR
OWN
HERE

15

5-STROKE ROLL

We've played singles and doubles. Now let's put them together. Can you guess how many notes the 5-Stroke Roll has in it? That's right, smartypants: five notes! Play a double (or two notes) with one hand, then another double (two more notes) with the other hand, and then one final single note with the hand that you started with. Easy as that!

When we begin with our right hand,
our 5-Stroke Roll will be played: R R L L R

Beginning with our left hand, it will be: L L R R L

Play all five notes even and steady from the first to the last, just like you would smoothly count the numbers "1 2 3 4 5." Pause and then repeat the roll again. Roll, pause, roll, pause, roll, pause, roll . . . over and over.

Rudi suggests switching which hand starts each time, so that you get really good playing them both ways.

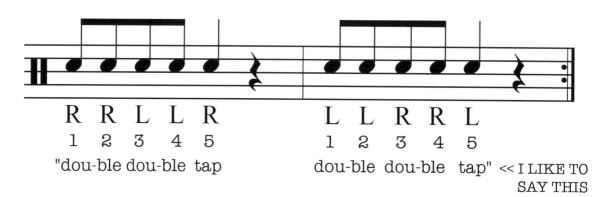

R R L L R
1 2 3 4 5
"dou-ble dou-ble tap

L L R R L
1 2 3 4 5
dou-ble dou-ble tap" << I LIKE TO
SAY THIS

ACCENTS

Quick break from our rolls to learn about a new
little tool that we get to start using.

This thing right here . . .

. . . is called an Accent.

When we're reading music and we see an accent
written above or below a note . . .

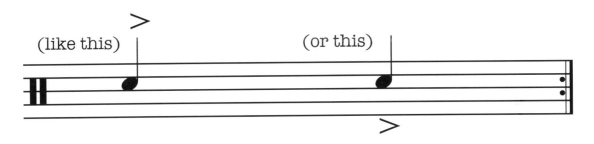

. . . it is telling us to accent (or accentuate) just
that note. How do we do that? By simply playing
that note louder than the other notes around it.

The easiest and best way to play that note louder
(or accent it) is by starting that stroke with our
stick tip in a higher position than we play our
other regular strokes from.

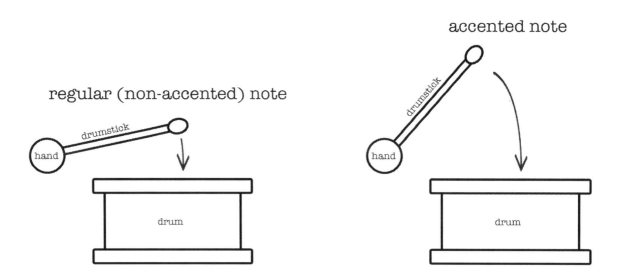

regular (non-accented) note

accented note

Don't lift your whole arm up in the air to get that stick tip higher. Just bend a bit more at the wrist and it will get right where you want it to be.

Try playing a few regular volume notes on your drum or pad, followed by some louder accented notes. Hear the difference? See the difference? Feel the difference?

Now let's go back and add an accent on the last note of each of our 5-Stroke Rolls! Remember to keep your stick tips low during the doubles strokes and raise only to strike that accented note that ends the phrase.

R   R   L   L   R   L   L   R   R   L

9-STROKE ROLL

That roll was cool and all, but now let's create a
longer one: the 9-Stroke Roll. All we have to do to play
it is add a couple more doubles at the beginning
of our pattern. Instead of two doubles, we now have
four doubles, plus one single tap at the very end.

Keep those notes even!

Like we did with the last roll, let's put
an accent on the last note.

17-STROKE ROLL

Ready for an EVEN LONGER one? Yeah? Okay, you
asked for it . . . here's the 17-Stroke Roll! Crazy, right?
It's long but actually easier than you might think.
You're going to be rocking this thing in no time.

Any chance you can already guess what it's going to be?

Our 5-Stroke Roll had two doubles plus a single tap.
Our 9-Stroke Roll had four doubles plus a single tap.
And our 17-Stroke Roll is going to have EIGHT doubles
plus a single tap. Did you guess correctly? Let's play it!

R R L L R R L L R R L L R R L L R

L L R R L L R R L L R R L L R R L

And with accents . . .

R R L L R R L L R R L L R R L L R

L L R R L L R R L L R R L L R R L

DIDDLE RUDIMENTS

Whew, incredible job on all of those. You now
know a total of seven rudiments!

I'm excited about this next section, because we get to
take our singles and doubles and combine them into
one of my all-time favorite words to say:
Paradiddles!

Can you say that? Paradiddle. Now say it four times.
Paradiddle, paradiddle, paradiddle, paradiddle.
Now say them faster . . . and again even faster!

Haha, did your tongue get tied up trying to spit that
out super fast? Mine always does. I love that word
and I love all of the paradiddle rudiments.
Let's get into them.

SINGLE PARADIDDLE

First up is the Single Paradiddle, which is made up of
two singles (R L) and then a double (R R).
Put them together - nice and steady,
of course - and we get: R L R R

That's a right paradiddle. A left paradiddle will be
played as the exact opposite of that, starting with
the left hand: L R L L

When we put the two paradiddle stickings above
together, back to back, we won't pause at all between
them. A right paradiddle flows straight into a left
paradiddle, which flows straight back into a
right paradiddle, and on and on and on.

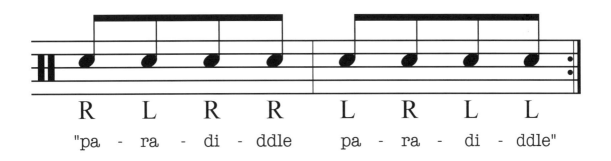

Don't let the doubles in these be played faster or
slower than the singles. Remember, no pauses between
any of the notes, and no speeding up or slowing down.

Those accents we used on our rolls . . . think
we could use them here, too? You bet we can!
This time, let's accent the very first note of every
Single Paradiddle.

Take your time and begin these very slowly. Make the
first note of each one loud (with the stick tip
starting from a high position), but keep the rest of them
softer (with the stick tips starting from a low position).

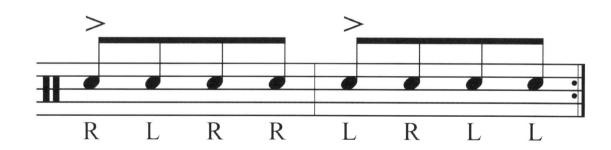

DOUBLE PARADIDDLE

Aren't paradiddles awesome? I definitely think so.

Another thing that's just as awesome is expanding on those and creating a longer paradiddle variation. To do that, let's add two more notes to play Double Paradiddles.

The two new notes we're adding will be single strokes that fall right in front of the four regular Single Paradiddle notes we've already been playing. One way to think about them is that they are simply four singles (alternating between our two hands) followed by a double (two notes with one hand).

Like before, our first Double Paradiddle starts with the right hand and the next one starts with the left. So instead of RLRR LRLL, we now get RLRLRR LRLRLL.

R L R L R R L R L R L L

It's accent time again! Just like you did with our Single Paradiddles, now make the very first note of each Double Paradiddle louder than all of the other notes.

Remember, the trick to make this easiest is starting every accented stroke from a high stick tip position, and starting every softer stroke from a low position.

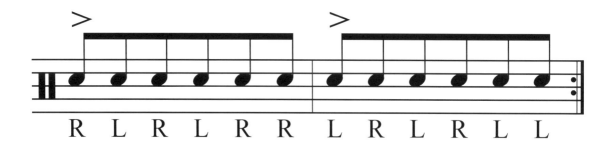

R L R L R R L R L R L L

Nice work. To make those even cooler than they already are, let's play TWO accents in every one of them! Here, we're going to accent the 1st and 3rd notes of each Double Paradiddle.

On the RLRLRR side, we'll accent both of the right hand singles, and on the LRLRLL side, we'll accent both of the left hand singles.

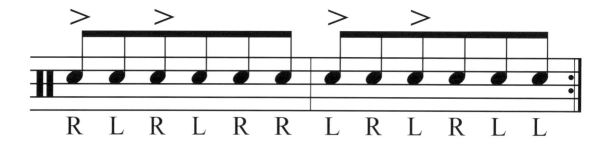

R L R L R R L R L R L L

Keep the loud notes loud and the soft notes soft. These should sound like:
LOUD soft LOUD soft soft soft - LOUD soft LOUD soft soft soft

Repeat them over and over again, and gradually speed them up once you feel comfortable.

TRIPLE PARADIDDLE

We've got Single Paradiddles and Double
Paradiddles . . . any clue what's next?
Correct you are, Triple Paradiddles!

To play Double Paradiddle, we added two single strokes
to the front of every Single Paradiddle. Now we're going
to add TWO MORE single strokes in front, so that our
Triple Paradiddles are six single strokes plus a
double stroke. This is a long one!

R L R L R L R R   L R L R L R L L

As always, keep these smooth and steady.
No goofy pauses or uneven notes.

Like we have with our other paradiddles, let's
accent the very first note of each Triple Paradiddle.

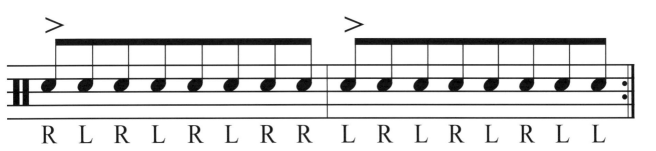

R L R L R L R R   L R L R L R L L

We played a Double Paradiddle variation that had two accents per hand in it. Now let's play a Triple Paradiddle variation that has THREE accents per hand!

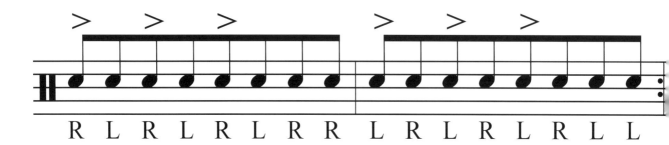

R L R L R L R R L R L R L R L L

How cool is that, right?!

I definitely hope you're having fun with these.
I know that I always do.

Take a second right now and check out what you've learned so far in this guide.

We've went over all of these rudiments:

- Single Stroke Roll
- Single Stroke Four
- Single Stroke Seven
- Double Stroke Roll
- 5-Stroke Roll
- 9-Stroke Roll
- 17-Stroke Roll
- Single Paradiddle
- Double Paradiddle
- Triple Paradiddle

Count all of those up to see how many you've learned.

Wait that's . . . 10!
You've gotten through exactly 10 rudiments,
which means you are officially halfway through
our 20 Essential Drum Rudiments.

Congratulations! Give yourself a pat on the back for
all of that hard work. You've earned it.

That's a lot of rudiments
learned – isn't this a ton
of fun?

Want to learn more?
Cool . . . onward to the
next page.

PARADIDDLE-DIDDLE

Rudi loves calling our next rudiment
Paraturtle-turtles or Paradiddle-turtles or
Paraturtle-diddles (whew, tongue twisters!).
I'm not so sure those names would catch on with
everybody else, but they ARE super silly and fun :)

For now, we'll stick with their regular name, the
equally fun to say Paradiddle-diddle!

When playing Paradiddle-diddles, instead of adding
singles strokes as we did with some of our other
paradiddle rudiments, we're going to add a double
stroke. Start with our basic Single Paradiddle (RLRR)
and add one more double stroke (LL) at the
very end, so that we now have: RLRRLL

Of course, we also need to be able to play the same
combination (two single strokes and two double
strokes) beginning with the left hand: LRLLRR

WARNING:
There is one huge
difference between all
of our other paradiddle
stickings and this crazy new
Paradiddle-diddle sticking.

Instead of switching back and forth between right hand and left hand starting each time . . .

RLRR **L**RLL

RLRLRR **L**RLRLL

RLRLRLRR **L**RLRLRLL

. . . the Paradiddle-diddle will usually be repeated with the same hand always staying in front. The LL sticking at the end of the right Paradiddle-diddle makes it natural to go straight back into another right Paradiddle-diddle.

R L R R L L   R L R R L L

Make sense?

In the exact same way, the RR sticking at the end of the left Paradiddle-diddle leads smoothly back into another left Paradiddle-diddle.

L R L L R R   L R L L R R

Excellent job with those two Paradiddle-diddle stickings. I'm sure you probably already know what's next . . . yep, adding accents!

Let's accent the first note of our right Paradiddle-diddles, keeping all the other notes nice and quiet.

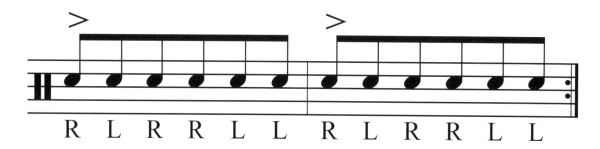

R L R R L L R L R R L L

And again with our left Paradiddle-diddles:

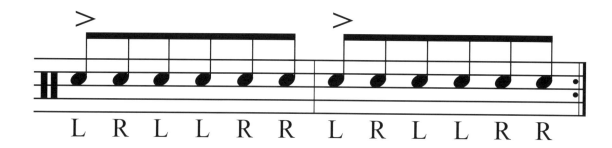

L R L L R R L R L L R R

MORE ROLL RUDIMENTS

So far, we've learned several Roll Rudiments and Diddle Rudiments. Before we move on to some completely new types of rudiments, we're going to first learn two more Roll Rudiments.

On all of our earlier rolls, we never played more than two notes at a time (or a "double") with each hand, before switching to the opposite hand. Well, that is about to change!

TRIPLE STROKE ROLL

The very first rudiment we learned in this guide was the Single Stroke Roll, which had each hand playing one note at a time. Then we moved to the Double Stroke Roll, which had each hand playing two notes at a time.

Going even further, we now get to learn the Triple Stroke Roll, which has each hand playing THREE notes at a time. And that's really all there is to it – three steady notes with the right hand, then three steady notes with the left hand, back to three with the right, then again with the left, and continue repeating.

We first saw "triplets" (three-note groupings) in our Single Stroke Four and Single Stroke Seven rudiments. The difference here is that, instead of alternating our hands between every note, we're playing three at a time with each hand before switching.

Focus on staying relaxed, always playing exactly three notes with each hand (no more and no fewer) and letting the flow of notes stay even and smooth.

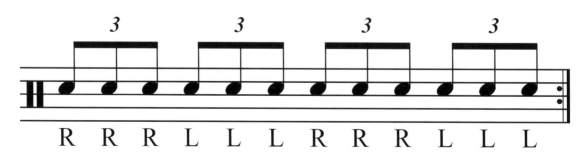

MULTIPLE BOUNCE ROLL

Are you ready for some serious fun? Suhweet! We're about to play the Multiple Bounce Roll, also sometimes called the Closed Roll or the Buzz Roll.

"The Buzz Roll?" you ask? Yep, this one gets that nickname because it sounds like you are playing one long, smooth, nonstop "buzz" on the snare drum. It's a tiny bit tricky to get it going at first, but we'll gradually put it together in three simple steps. Here we go . . .

STEP 1: ONE HAND AT A TIME

Start with only your right hand. Just like playing a single stroke, bend at the wrist, hitting the pad or drum once and then letting the stick tip pull away, like normal.

Only play one note? Good, that is a single stroke. We've done lots of those so far in this guide. Now let's do something very different from that: a multiple bounce stroke (or a buzz).

Hit the pad or drum again, still bending at the wrist, and still always staying in control of your drumstick by keeping it held securely between your thumb and index finger. But this time, instead of pulling the stick tip away, let your hand stay down, and allow the drumstick to bounce (as many times as it naturally wants to) on the drumhead.

Instead of a Single Stroke . . .

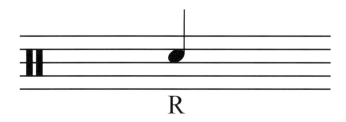

. . . you get a Multiple Bounce . . .

. . . usually written like that, with a little "z" on the note. It will sound sort of like:

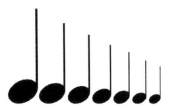

Don't force too many notes in there by playing more than once with your wrist. Relax, let the stick bounce and, with only one wrist motion, you can create several notes on the drum.
You just played a buzz!

Take your time and practice that over and over again, until you feel comfortable getting those multiple bounces from that one wrist action.

Rrrrrrr Rrrrrrr Rrrrrrr Rrrrrrr

It's your left hand's turn!
Try getting that buzz from just one wrist stroke.

Lllllll

Practice those until they feel good and sound good.

L LLLLLL L LLLLLL L LLLLLL L LLLLLL

Good to go with both hands?
Fantastic! Let's move on.

STEP 2: PUTTING THE HANDS TOGETHER

Since we can now play multiple bounces with each hand separately, we'll now put them both together. To start doing that, let's play a buzz with the right stick, then leave a short pause (or a "rest"), then play a buzz with the left stick, then leave another pause, and then go back to the beginning and do it all over again.

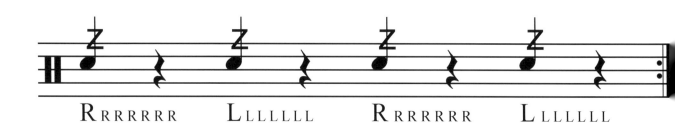

R RRRRRR   L LLLLLL   R RRRRRR   L LLLLLL

Don't be in a hurry.
Leave some silent space between each buzz you play.
Can you make every one of them sound the same?
Do your rights and lefts sound alike?

Onward to . . .

STEP 3: OVERLAPPING THE BUZZES

So much nice work in those last two steps. You rock!

We are super close to playing our full-on, official
Multiple Bounce Roll. Only two things left to do.
Here we're going to remove the pauses (rests)
and put our buzzes back to back.

Just as one buzz is naturally ending, let the other
hand start into its buzz.

R RRRRRR L LLLLLL   R RRRRRR L LLLLLL

As the right stick comes to a stop, the left stick takes
over. Then back to the right. Then left, right, left, etc.
We no longer have rests, just a steady stream of
buzzes being played right after another.

The last thing we're going to do with these is to go
beyond even just playing them back to back,
and start overlapping them.

As you get the hang of our last exercise, now try to
STOP waiting until one stick is completely done before
the next one starts. For example, just a few notes
before the right stick has quit bouncing on the
drumhead, the left stick can now jump in, so that its
notes have started up before the right stick has
totally stopped. The same goes for the next right:
it gets to jump in again before the left has stopped.

R RRRRRRRRRR   R RRRRRRRRRR
    L LLLLLLLLLL   L LLLLLLLLLL

And there is the Multiple Bounce Roll! Relax as you
work on this. As Rudi mentioned earlier, don't rush.
Also, try to make both hands sound the same.
We don't want one playing louder than the other,
or one being tense and choppy.

With practice, all of the notes you're playing will
turn into one long, smooth, continuous buzz.
Hear how they all blend nicely into each other?
Now THAT, my friend, is an awesome little drum roll!

FLAM RUDIMENTS

Another silly-sounding rudiment name for you:

Flam!

Say that one five times fast:
flam, flam, flam, flam, flam.

Notice the way your tongue almost rolls as you
say the first two letters of that word? That's kind of
how this rudiment is going to sound when it's
played. Here, let us show you how . . .

FLAM

A right flam (the first we'll learn) is written in music like this:

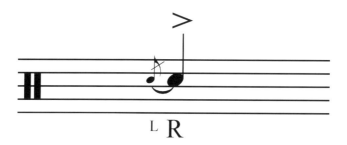

L R

The right stroke is the main stroke, a regular volume (or loud) note played by that hand. But there are a few new things happening with that left stroke.

1. It's really small.

2. It's crossed out.

3. It appears just before the right stroke, connected by a little swooping line (which we call a "tie").

That all seems like a lot to figure out but I'll make it quick and easy for you. All it means is that our left stroke is going to be played very softly, and falls just a split second before our louder right stroke (ALMOST at the exact same time, but not quite).

The louder main stroke can also be written with an accent above it, which we've done here, as a reminder that that note is played louder than the other small, soft note (often called a "grace note").

Our starting stick positions are the most important things to get right as we kick into these. To prepare to play a right flam, get your drumsticks into the following starting positions.

The left stick should be held flat and level above the drum (or "parallel" to the drumhead), with the stick tip only about an inch away from the drumhead. Bending at the right wrist, bring the right stick tip up to a higher position, pointing that stick either straight up or close to it.

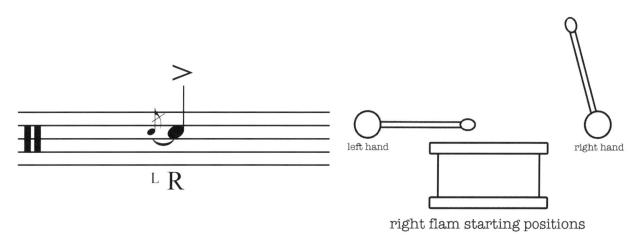

right flam starting positions

When those are in the correct spots, start the sticks into motion toward the drumhead at the same time. Both wrists move as if they're connected – one just happens to be closer to the drum than the other. Make sense?

The left tip should strike first, creating a really soft tap sound, and then stop moving in the same low position it had started in. Barely after that, the right tip comes down, playing a louder note, and then returns right back to the high position it started in.

You just played your first flam! Go ahead and play another one. Can you hear how the sound is similar to the rudiment's name?

Keep working on those right flams, leaving some space between each of them, but making sure that the two notes of each flam stay super close together.

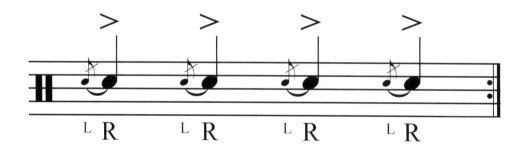

We can't forget left flams! Here are our starting positions: Hold the right stick low and flat above the drum, with the stick tip about an inch from the drumhead. Bend the left wrist to bring the left stick tip up to our high position.

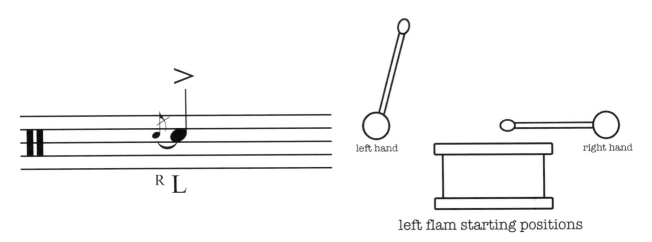

left hand

right hand

left flam starting positions

Again, both sticks move toward the drum together but hit just a tiny bit apart from each other. A soft right note is played first, following immediately by a louder left note. Both stick tips should stop in their original starting positions.

Play your left flams over and over again, with some space between each. Remember to make the two sticks hit at ALMOST the same time. Not EXACTLY the same time, but oh so close.

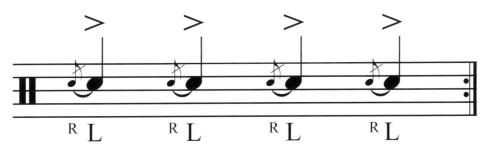

I bet $5 you know what's next.
You got it, combining them!

To play alternating flams, there's only one little change we're going to make. We're going to change where each stick stops after each flam is played.

Do you remember how we said that after our right flam we should end in that same right flam starting position? Similar for the left. Well, that's what we're changing for our alternating flams.

After playing a RIGHT flam, practice ending in the starting position for a LEFT flam. That puts you into the perfect position to play that next upcoming flam. After playing that next (LEFT) flam, stop your sticks in the RIGHT flam starting position. Again, you're now already all set to continue on to our next alternated flam.

Take these SLOWLY and practice, practice, practice!

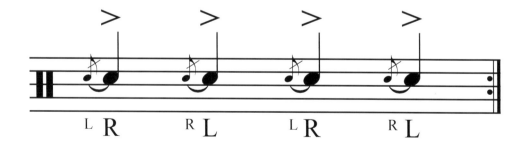

FLAM TAP

Flams are sometimes played by themselves but are also used within lots of other rudiments. Flam Taps are a good example. They are nothing more than what the name suggests they are . . .
a flam followed by a tap (single stroke).

The sticking is simply:
a right flam + a right tap + a left flam + a left tap

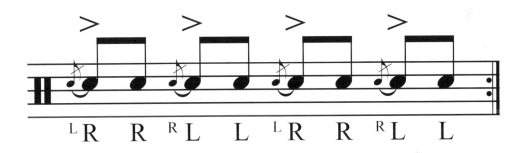

Another way we can look at these is that they are a Double Stroke Roll with a Flam on the first note of each double. Do you see that?

FLAM ACCENT

Triplets popped up in a few of our earlier rudiments. How many notes in a triplet? Yes, three!

For the fun of it, let's play some triplets – alternating hands (RLR LRL) and accenting the first note of each triplet grouping. Keep them smooth, with no pauses between the groupings.

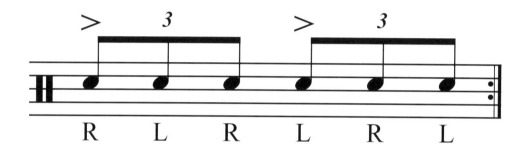

Nice! Our newest rudiment, the Flam Accent, consists of triplet groupings just like those above, with the first note of each turned into a flam.

right flam + left tap + right tap +
left flam + right tap + left tap

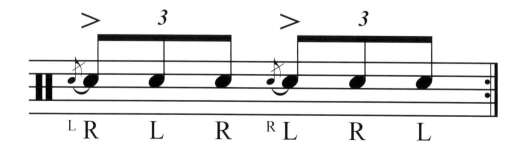

SWISS ARMY TRIPLETS

One more flam rudiment for you. These are called
Swiss Army Triplets, or sometimes just
Swiss Triplets for short.

They are super similar to the Flam Accents but use a
slightly different sticking pattern. Instead of always
alternating like we did before (RLR LRL), this time
play our triplets using a combination of TWO right
strokes and ONE left stroke. Don't forget an accent
on the first note of each triplet group!

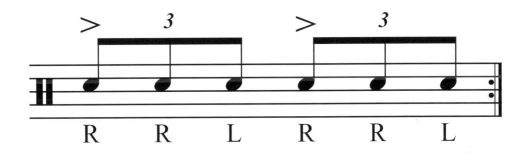

Now turn the first note of each grouping into a
flam . . . and we're playing Swiss Army Triplets!

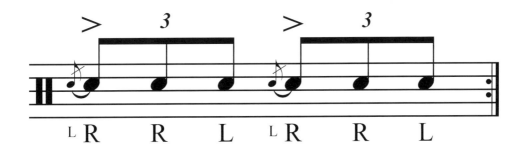

Since these have a right flam in front every single time, we also need to try playing them with the opposite sticking, so that we can practice having the left flam in front.

First start with accented triplets played with TWO left strokes and ONE right stroke . . .

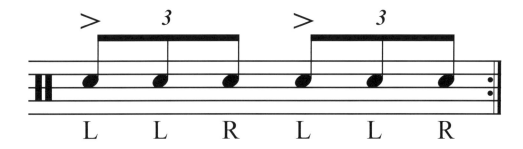

. . . and then turn those accents into flams!

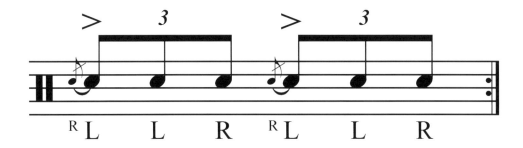

DRAG RUDIMENTS

This last section of the guide focuses on using "drags," which are somewhat like the flams we learned in the last section. The big difference is that – instead of playing a small, low, quiet grace note right before our louder, main stroke – we play TWO of them!

These are Rudi's favorite rudiments, so he wants me to hurry up (for a change) and show them to you. We'd better dive in!

DRAG

Let's get set to play a right drag.
It's written like this:

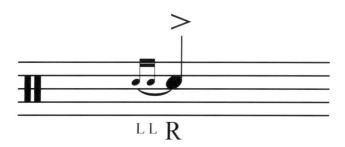

L L R

Notice that there are TWO small left grace notes up front. Those are tied to a big, primary right stroke (sometimes accented like we have done here).

Our starting positions are exactly the same as the starting positions we used for right flams. As a reminder, here it is:

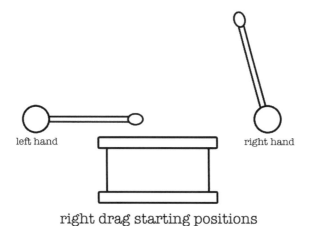

left hand   right hand

right drag starting positions

When we play these, we'll first hit two times with that low left stick tip. Keep those two strokes very soft and fairly fast. Just after those two left notes are played, we add one accented stroke played with the right stick, coming down from its high starting position.

Both stick tips move toward the drum at the same time. The left is closer, so hits first, but barely. There is not really a pause before the right stick hits. All three notes end up sounding super close together, one right after another.

A quick little flourish of two soft strokes + one loud stroke = a drag!

Take your time and practice right drags over and over again. Keep the three notes of each drag close together but leave some space between each new drag that you play.

It's the left drag's turn. Once again, same starting position we used on left flams:

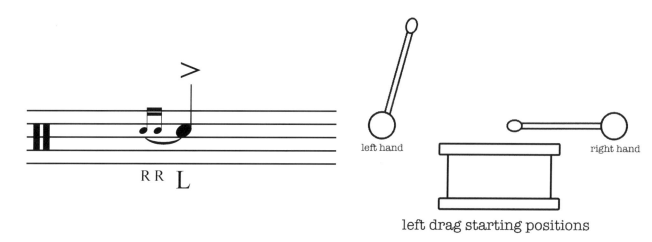

left hand

right hand

left drag starting positions

RR L

This time our right hand will play two soft grace notes, immediately followed by one accented left stroke. Play slowly and keep the right stick tip low, but bring the left stick tip back up to its high position.

Practice these (with a space between each drag) until they're really comfortable for you.

RR L   RR L   RR L   RR L

Okay, now let's do some alternating drags, playing a right drag, then a left drag, then right, then left, and on and on.

Begin in the starting position for a RIGHT drag. However, this time, after playing our right drag, we're going to end in position to play a LEFT drag (left stick tip UP, right stick tip DOWN). We'll then play a left drag and (you guessed it!) end in the right drag position.

Make sure you're in the perfectly correct position for each upcoming drag before going ahead and playing it. Take your time, pause between each and get those starting positions just right. Give your hands time to memorize these movements.

REMINDER FROM RUDI:

The longer you keep every one of these rudiments
super slow, relaxed and perfect RIGHT NOW,
the better and faster you'll have them LATER ON.

Drummers who practice fast, tense and sloppy
just train themselves to ALWAYS play tense
and sloppy. Don't be that drummer. Instead, train
yourself to always play relaxed and perfectly.

DRAG PARADIDDLE #1

Combining two cool rudiments can only create another rudiment that's even cooler, right? That's totally the case with Drag Paradiddle #1.

This one starts off with an accented single stroke, followed by a paradiddle that has its first note turned into a drag! Crazy, huh? I love this one – let's do it!

First comes an accented note with the right stick. Then we play a right drag (two quiet little left strokes + a louder right stroke). But the RIGHT that's played as part of that drag is ALSO the first note of the right paradiddle we need to play, so after that, we just wrap it up with a left-right-right.

Of course, we also need to be able to play the same rudiment starting with our other hand. For that, we begin with an accented note with the left stick. That's followed by a left drag (rrL), finishing off our left paradiddle with a right-left-left.

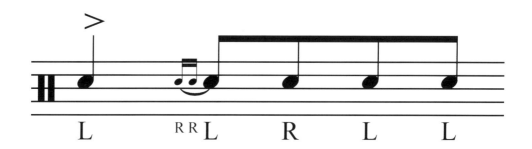

And now it's time to do WHAT?
Yeah, you know the drill . . .
it's time to put both of these together.

Play a right Drag Paradiddle #1 followed by a left Drag Paradiddle #1, and voilá, you've done it!
Simple, simple.

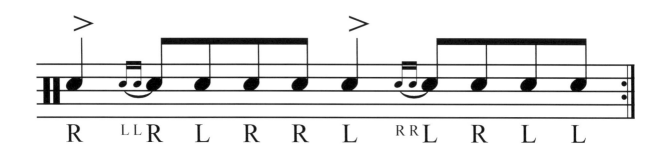

SINGLE RATAMACUE

The next drag rudiment we'll work on is also
a fun one to say, and like the last one,
it's a combination of two other rudiments
that we already know how to play.

A Single Ratamacue is really just a Single Stroke Four
(the second rudiment you learned in this guide)
that has its first note turned into a drag, and its last
note accented. Say the word "Ratamacue." Okay now
say it again but, this time, roll the letter "R" on your
tongue – as if you're trying to sound like a motor
running, or a cat purring – and say the last syllable
("cue") louder than the others. It can be tricky but
when saying it like that . . . RrrratamaCUE . . .
its name sounds pretty much the way the rudiment
will sound when we play it! And I think it's way
more fun to say it that way, anyway :)

Let's get to it.

Start with a right drag (llR) followed
immediately by three more single strokes (l-r-l).

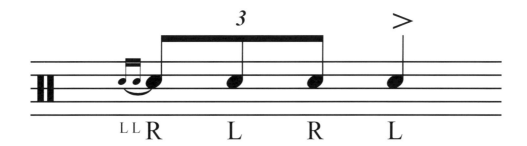

And you KNOW that we're going to play that with the opposite sticking, too, so we might as well hit that right away here.

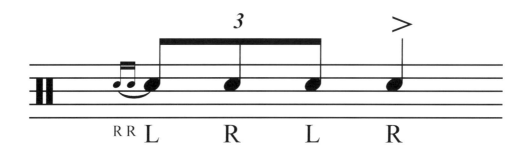

Combination time, once again:

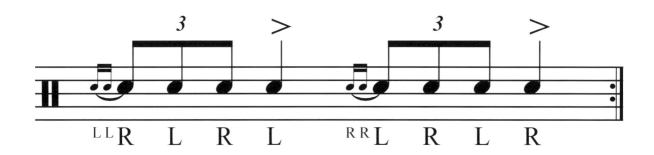

Repeat over and over again,
and BAM – you've got it!

Holy smokes, you just learned your
20th drum rudiment! Can you believe it?

Rudi and I are impressed by how fast you worked
your way through all of these. To celebrate, you
can get your very own certificate of completion at:
SlamminSimon.com/RudimentCertificate

Print it off, add your name, and please send us
a photo of you showing it off! You can even frame it
and put it up on your wall to show family, friends and
other drummers your awesome accomplishment!

Remember that LEARNING rudiments is only
the first step. Next, you should:

• practice them every single day, to memorize
them and gradually get them more comfortable and
relaxed, cleaner and smoother sounding, and faster.

• mix them up to make up your own
combinations and drum solos!

Thanks for reading, and for letting me and Rudi share all of these rudiments with you. When you get a chance, message us at **slamminsimon@gmail.com** and let us know what you thought about this guide.

We look forward to hearing from you!

If you'd like a cool poster of me, Rudi and all 20 Essential Drum Rudiments, visit: **SlamminSimon.com/RudimentPoster**

Also, check out our other guides at **SlamminSimon.com** to learn even more super awesome drum rudiments, grooves and fills.

You rock!

Slammin' X
Simon

Made in the USA
Columbia, SC
05 September 2021